BY CAMEL OR BY CAR

A LOOK AT TRANSPORTATION
BY GUY BILLOUT

Copyright © 1979 by Guy Billout
Library of Congress Cataloging in Publications Data
Billout, Guy. By Camel Or By Car.
Summary: Text and illustrations describe 16 types of water, air, and land transportation.
1. Transportation-Juvenile Literature (1. Transportation)
I. Title. TA1149. B54 1979 380.5 78/26120
ISBN 0/13/109603/6   0/13/109595/1(pbk.)

10 9 8 7 6 5 4 3

PRENTICE-HALL, INC.
ENGLEWOOD CLIFFS, NEW JERSEY

CAMEL

The camel has been around for more than 3,500 years. About six and a half feet high, it weighs between 1,000 pounds and 1,500 pounds. Able to carry 350 to 450 pounds in load weight, it can cover 40 miles a day. The camel has adapted remarkably well to its harsh environment where water is scarce. It can go for a week without water and for ten days without food. Camels can live to be 50 years old.

There were no palm trees and sand dunes where I grew up, but the camel was a familiar figure from the manger that was built in the church to celebrate Christmas. As children, we eagerly awaited the arrival of the three wise men to join the holy family and the ox, the ass and the shepherds with their sheep. The three wise men were magnificent in their rich clothes, carrying their wonderful gifts, but the fascination for me was the camels: unlike the other characters in the nativity scene, all drawn towards the new-born baby, the camels, with their haughty expressions seemed set apart from the others.

BICYCLE

In 1791, the Comte de Sivrac of France built the first bicycle. It was called the Célérifère. Propelled by the feet, it had no brakes or steering. Today, a ten-speed bicycle has a 17″ to 25″ frame with 27″ wheels, and weighs 20 to 40 pounds. A powerful rider can go up to 45 miles an hour. In 1973, a man on a bicycle reached the speed of 140 miles an hour behind a pace car. A bicycle can last 15 years.

When I was a child, I believed that bicycles stayed upright because the air moving around the machine and its rider was holding them up, as two pieces of bread surround a sandwich. One day at a fair, I saw a man riding a bicycle in what seemed a motionless fashion. Getting closer, I discovered that the bicycle was on a set of rollers. The man was pedalling, the wheels were turning, but nothing was holding up the machine and its rider. If I could not figure out the phenomenon, I did understand that I had to give up my former theory.

MOTORCYCLE

Pierre and Ernest Michaux built the first motorcycle in Paris in 1869. It was powered by steam. A modern, all-purpose motorcycle runs on premium gasoline and can go 50 to 55 miles per gallon, with a range of 110 to 125 miles with a full tank of gas. It can reach speeds of 80 to 90 miles an hour. Weighing 270 to 320 pounds, it can carry much more than its own weight—400 pounds!

My father took me for my first motorcycle ride when I was five. It was a frustrating experience . . . we just went around the block! As I found out later, gasoline, along with many other things, was in short supply because the war had just ended in Europe. And besides, I had three sisters and one brother . . . all waiting for their turn.

CAR

Because no other means of transportation offers its flexibility, the car has become a way of life. A full-sized American car weighs 3,250 pounds. It can carry a load of 1,000 pounds and reach speeds up to 100 miles an hour, with a fuel consumption of 16 to 23 miles per gallon. For all the marvels of technology that have created the car, it is remarkably inefficient in one way: only ten per cent of its fuel energy is converted into motion. The average life span of modern cars is five to six years.

When my father bought a car, the family went on frequent trips to the country. Invariably, we returned home by night. For me, that was the best part of the trip. I would imagine that it was the middle of a cold winter night and we were crossing a very large forest where people were attacked by bandits (a true story that happened to a neighbor: he escaped unharmed and came to our house to report ... to the great delight of the children!) Suddenly, a terrible storm struck. The rain beating against the windows and the moaning of the wipers would induce me to sleep. As the car entered town, my mother would awaken us and I would have to face the dreadful prospect of getting out of the car.

TRUCK

A truck can carry 50,000 to 60,000 pounds of cargo. It runs on diesel fuel. It has a 250 horsepower engine that can pull the truck along at a maximum speed of 68 to 70 miles an hour, but it only gets four miles per gallon of fuel. A truck can travel an average distance of 400,000 miles before its engine must be replaced and 800,000 miles before the truck itself wears out.

Coming from Europe, I have been bewildered by some facts of American life. One of these is the form of modern piracy that is the hijacking of trucks and their cargo. One day, looking down on traffic from a second-story window, I noticed big numbers painted on the top of truck trailers. I learned that these big numbers help the police helicopters track down stolen trucks.

BUS

A horse-drawn vehicle, run in Paris in 1662, can be considered the ancestor of the modern bus. Typically 48 feet long, weighing 18,000 pounds, a bus can carry 53 seated passengers at a maximum speed of 62 miles an hour. In the United States, buses have gradually replaced the train as cheap, reliable means of transportation. A bus can last fifteen years.

When going to camp, the children of my neighborhood would travel by chartered bus. We usually left at night, to arrive in the middle of the following day after numerous rest stops by the side of the road. I remember the smell of the exhaust fumes from the bus engine on these stops. I liked that smell because it reminded me of the excitement of going to camp. Since then I have lived in big cities, where buses just smell bad.

SUBWAY

The subway is the most efficient means of public transportation in big cities, because it travels underground. A subway train is made up of several interconnected cars, each one with four motors which run on electricity picked up from a special rail on the side of the tracks, and delivers 400 horsepower. Each car can accomodate 76 seated passengers and four times as many as that during rush hours, when people stand. The subway car lasts as long as 25 to 30 years.

The greatest treat for me, or any child growing up in a small French town, was to go to Paris. There the most exciting things to do were to climb the Eiffel Tower and to ride the Metro, the Paris subway. The Metro is known for the huge advertising posters that cover the walls of the stations. One of these posters was showing a pink cow on top of a soap made with milk. That cow made famous a poster artist (Savignac is his name) whose work, later on, was my first and most important influence as a commercial artist.

TRAIN

A railroad train is made up of a number of cars which can carry either passengers or cargo. In the United States, the typical diesel-electric locomotive weighs 250,000 pounds; using diesel fuel, it develops 2,500 horsepower enabling it to exert 75,000 pounds of pull on a train averaging 80 miles an hour. Railroad equipment can last 40 years. The first commercial locomotive was built in 1804 by Richard Trevithick in England.

As a boy growing up in the forties I knew the last steam locomotives, and I remember them as haunting images. At that time in France, the railroad station was huge, even in a small city, with a vast cast iron and glass roof that covered the platforms and tracks. I would look intently at the end of the tracks where they disappeared into the horizon line, and suddenly, without a noise, the black machine appeared. Little by little the panting of the steam engine became distinct, punctuated by the blows of the steam whistle. When the tall, frightening machine entered under the station roof in a cloud of smoke, the noise echoed in the monumental space. In this overwhelming display of the engine's power, the brakes started to scream, bringing the train to a full stop. Today I am sometimes taken by surprise by the slick and almost silent arrival of electric trains.

SNOWMOBILE

The snowmobile is propelled on snow by a rubber-cleated tread driven by an engine which uses a combination of oil and gasoline as fuel and can deliver 26 horsepower. Two skis on the front of the vehicle allow steering. Used as transportation in rural areas, it is also used for sport. The snowmobile can reach a speed of up to 85 to 105 miles an hour. The machine lasts about ten years.

Having always been interested in machines, I believed I knew most existing means of transportation. Coming to the United States, I discovered the snowmobile, never having seen one even in pictures. Doing research for this book, I learned that the snowmobile was invented in the late twenties, and found it interesting that man learned to fly long before he found a motorized way to ride on snow.

SHIP

Today, the biggest supertanker is a ship weighing 553,000 tons, deadweight. It can transport up to 160 million gallons of crude oil. It is a descendant of a ship named *Great Britain,* which was the first iron-hulled steamer powered by a screw propeller. It crossed the Atlantic Ocean in 1843. Using high-viscosity fuel for its turbine engines, it generates 65,000 horsepower that can propel the ship at sixteen knots. Fully loaded, it takes more than three miles for it to come to a complete stop. Most supertankers are built to last about ten years.

As a child, I knew a lullaby that went:

> Tell me, Mother,
> Do boats on the water have legs?
> No, no, silly dear,
> If they did, they would walk.

I guess I was that silly one, since I could not figure out how huge steel ships could stay afloat when the tiniest stone would sink right down to the bottom.

BALLOON

The first passengers of a hot air balloon were a cock, a duck and a sheep. People followed shortly afterward aboard a captive balloon, ascending 50 feet above the ground on October 15, 1783. A modern hot air balloon uses bottled propane gas in burners placed under the opening of the balloon-shaped bag to heat the air. It can reach an altitude of up to 130,000 feet and can travel over 1,500 miles from where it left the ground.

When I was a student, I had a pad of writing paper that had a Montgolfière on its cover. Since I saw this picture every day, I just took it for granted, as a strange decorative drawing. Later on, I learned it was the very first balloon to take off with men on board. The balloon was named after the two Montgolfier brothers who invented it in 1783. They were directors of a paper mill, which was still manufacturing the paper I used in school!

AERIAL TRAM

The typical aerial tram is a cabin five feet wide and twelve feet long. It can hold as many as 126 passengers. The car moves along an aerial cable which is supported by towers called pylons. A 1600 horsepower electric motor at the end of the cable moves the car at a maximum speed of sixteen miles an hour. The highest aerial tramway in the world is in the mountains of Venezuela—the car can climb 15,000 feet above the ground.

What I enjoy most about riding an aerial tram is the moment when the car draws near one of the pylons that hold the cable. At first there is the feeling that the car speeds up as it climbs its way to the top of the pylon. The car trembles as it passes the pylon, and for a second I feel as though the car is plunging in the abyss, but then it resumes its silent flight to the next pylon . . . .

PLANE

The jumbo jet Boeing 747 has become the symbol of today's jet travel, because its formidable size can accommodate between 330 and 490 passengers, helping to keep costs of travel down. The four turbofan engines deliver a total of 175,000 pounds of thrust, consuming kerosene. Its cruising speed is 555 miles an hour, with a 6,000 mile range. The first 747 jumbo jet, built in 1969, is still in use.

Just after the Second World War, I discovered a large piece of corrugated aluminum with a painted sign on it. It turned out to be a piece of military aircraft, and the sign was a German black cross. I was moved by my first encounter with a real airplane, as fragmented as it was. I was even more impressed when I learned that the plane had been shot down just a few years before.

HELICOPTER

The first helicopter was invented by Paul Cornu. His machine rose five feet up into the air on November 13, 1907. A modern helicopter, like the one shown in the picture, weighs 12,600 pounds, fully loaded. Using gasoline for fuel, its engine develops 1,450 horsepower with a range of 391 miles. The maximum speed is 132 miles an hour. A helicopter usually lasts for ten to fifteen years. Because of their expensive maintenance helicopters are mostly used for short trips, but no other machine can replace them for rescue work or for reaching otherwise inaccessible places.

In the late forties, when I was in elementary school, our teacher announced one morning that a helicopter had landed near our town. It was such an important event that all the schools around gathered at the site of the landing. All the children lined up in pairs to walk down a long road shaded by plane trees. At the end of the road, behind the last plane tree, was the magnificent machine: a glass bubble with a long, tubular tail. The helicopter did not take off in front of us, but we felt spoiled enough by this very unusual break in the boring school life.

SPACESHIP

The lunar module (LM), as shown in the picture is a small spaceship, carried from Earth by a huge Saturn rocket weighing 6.26 million pounds and delivering at the start of the flight 7.5 million pounds of thrust, burning liquid oxygen and refined kerosene. The LM is a two unit vessel with independent engines. To land on the Moon, the first unit delivers 9,900 pounds of thrust. It is left behind when the second unit takes off with 3,500 pounds of thrust, to meet the command module in orbit around the Moon. Its work done, the LM is abandoned and crashes onto the Moon. The command module alone returns to Earth.

A few months after I arrived in the United States, the first man landed on the Moon. As I was aware of the solemnity of the event, I was also wondering how the astronauts go to the bathroom. Later on, I was told that it is the most frequent question asked by visitors at the Air and Space museum of the Smithsonian in Washington D.C. The answer is not simple, and after going through detailed technical explanations, I remembered a few points: it takes close to an hour to do what five minutes would take in normal gravity. On the Apollo mission, urine was dumped into space, where it instantly flashes into ice crystals. When using their space suits, astronauts wear diapers.